NATIVE AMERICAN LIFE

Native American
Horsemanship

CLARISSA AYKROYD

Senior Consulting Editor Dr. Troy Johnson
Professor of History and American Indian Studies
California State University

MASON CREST PUBLISHERS • PHILADELPHIA

NATIVE AMERICAN LIFE

Mason Crest Publishers
370 Reed Road
Broomall PA 19008
www.masoncrest.com

First printing

1 3 5 7 9 8 6 4 2

Library of Congress Cataloging-in-Publication Data
on file at the Library of Congress

ISBN 1-59084-121-2

Frontispiece: A Crow chief rides confidently along the range
carrying his spear in this painting by Charles M. Russell.

Table of Contents

Introduction

For hundreds of years the dominant image of the Native American has been that of a stoic warrior, often wearing a full-length eagle feather headdress, riding a horse in pursuit of the buffalo, or perhaps surrounding some unfortunate wagon train filled with innocent west-bound American settlers. Unfortunately there has been little written or made available to the general public to dispel this erroneous generalization. This misrepresentation has resulted in an image of native people that has been translated into books, movies, and television programs that have done little to look deeply into the native worldview, cosmology, and daily life. Not until the 1990 movie *Dances with Wolves* were native people portrayed as having a human persona. For the first time, native people could express humor, sorrow, love, hate, peace, and warfare. For the first time native people could express themselves in words other than "ugh" or "Yes, Kemo Sabe." This series has been written to provide a more accurate and encompassing journey into the world of the Native Americans.

When studying the native world of the Americas, it is extremely important to understand that there are few "universals" that apply across tribal boundaries. With over 500 nations and 300 language groups the worlds of the Native Americans were diverse. The traditions of one group may or may not have been shared by neighboring groups. Sports, games, dance, subsistence patterns, clothing, and religion differed—greatly in some instances. And although nearly all native groups observed festivals and ceremonies necessary to insure the renewal of their worlds, these too varied greatly.

Of equal importance to the breaking down of old myopic and stereotypic images is that the authors in this series credit Native

Americans with a sense of agency. Contrary to the views held by the Europeans who came to North and South America and established the United States, Canada, Mexico, and other nations, some Native American tribes had sophisticated political and governing structures—that of the member nations of the Iroquois League, for example. Europeans at first denied that native people had religions but rather "worshiped the devil," and demanded that Native Americans abandon their religions for the Christian worldview. The readers of this series will learn that native people had well-established religions, led by both men and women, long before the European invasion began in the 16th and 17th centuries.

Gender roles also come under scrutiny in this series. European settlers in the northeastern area of the present-day United States found it appalling that native women were "treated as drudges" and forced to do the men's work in the agricultural fields. They failed to understand, as the reader will see, that among this group the women owned the fields and scheduled the harvests. Europeans also failed to understand that Iroquois men were diplomats and controlled over one million square miles of fur-trapping area. While Iroquois men sat at the governing council, Iroquois clan matrons caucused with tribal members and told the men how to vote.

These are small examples of the material contained in this important series. The reader is encouraged to use the extended bibliographies provided with each book to expand his or her area of specific interest.

Dr. Troy Johnson
Professor of History and American Indian Studies
California State University

1 The Village of Horses

Around the year 1750, anyone walking on the Great Plains of the central United States could have seen a Native American village from far off. The tribes of the Plains moved their villages of **tepees**, tall pointed structures, with them as they followed the herds of buffalo across the land. The tepees were the most obvious feature of the native village. But if that observer decided to come closer, he or she might have noticed something else. In many ways, the Plains village was a village of horses.

A Native American gazes over the plains from the back of his mount. Horses and the ability to ride well were very important to the Plains Indians.

The horses were somewhat small, but they were strong and fast. Some of them were kept in the village, tied with a rope to a peg outside a tepee, waiting to be mounted, or displaying a fine saddlecloth that one of the members of the tribe had recently made. The horses had a right to be in the village. They helped to move the tepees and all the people's goods. However, the village's main herd was located some distance away, watched over by boys. They guarded the herd to prevent raiders

A young boy works with an older man to break a pony's spirit in this illustration by Frederic Remington. Native American boys learned to ride at an early age. Often, boys were expert riders by the time they were five or six years old.

from stealing their best horses. They also drove the horses to a place where they could drink. As the horses drank, the boys stroked the younger ones to get them used to humans.

Elsewhere, a group of hunters was out on the plain, chasing down the buffalo on horseback. The horses dodged and swerved, leaping away from the dangerous horns and hooves of the big animals. In the days after a successful hunt, when they had plenty of food, the hunters might race their horses near the village. And in some quiet place, a boy might be working to **break** a young horse for riding.

In different areas of North America, as well as in South America, the native peoples had different uses for the horse. Most often, they used it for war, for hunting, and for transportation. They also used it for pleasure and in some forms of worship. For 200 years or more, the horse meant wealth, power, and freedom to many native tribes.

However, the horse was a relative newcomer to the American continent. An ancestor of the horse existed in the Americas tens of thousands of years before the continents were populated by humans, but these creatures had vanished a long time ago. In the 1500s, the horse made a return to America. Its arrival was part of the Spanish invasion of the New World. ဢ

2 The Coming of the "Sky Dogs"

In 1519, 11 ships sailed from Cuba for Mexico, carrying a large army under the leadership of Hernán Cortés. Cortés was a *conquistador*, a war leader who helped claim parts of the Americas for Spain. He would probably not have been so successful without the other passengers on his ships: 16 horses.

The Spanish started bringing horses to the West Indies in 1494. During the next 25 years, they set up breeding farms on the islands of Hispaniola, Jamaica, and Cuba. They knew how useful the horse could be in their attempt to take over the Americas. The horse allowed them to travel faster and take more *provisions* with them. Soon, they also found out that it made them more powerful in battle—partly because the Native Americans were frightened by their first sight of horses.

The Spanish explorer and conquistador Hernán Cortés rides into the Aztec capital, Tenochtitlán, in 1519. Before the arrival of the Spaniards in the Americas during the early years of the 16th century, the horse was unknown to Native Americans.

Bernal Díaz del Castillo, one of the soldiers who went with Cortés, described the reaction of the native Mexicans to the horseback riders: "[They] thought that the horse and its rider were all one animal, for they had never seen horses up to this time." At first, the natives must have thought that the horse was a type of dog. After they began to use the horse, they gave it names meaning "sky dog," "elk dog," or "big dog."

The horses that the Spanish brought to the Americas were primarily of a breed that still exists today, called the Andalusian. The Andalusian is fairly small, but strong. It developed from a combination of native Spanish breeds and the Barb horse. During the 700s, Muslims from North Africa had conquered most of Spain, bringing the Barb horse with them.

After about two years, Cortés and his men took Tenochtitlán, the capital of the Aztec empire. Once the Spanish had established themselves in Mexico, they used Indians as slaves to build **missions** so that they could convert the Native Americans to Christianity. Later, they also had them build missions along the Río Grande Valley in New Mexico. The missions included farms where the Spanish could breed horses. Soon, the Spanish started teaching the natives about horses, in particular, so they could help with the herds of cattle on the farms. Some of the natives left the missions, taking horses and their new knowledge of the animals with them. Tribes also raided the missions for horses. However, they did not always round up all of the horses set free during a raid. Soon, there were herds of **mustangs** in the wild, which the

The horse gave Spanish soldiers a great advantage
as they battled Native Americans in Mexico, South
America, and the American south and west. The
Aztecs and Incas believed that horses were
supernatural creatures that could not be killed.

15

A rider sits atop an Andalusian horse. Spanish conquistadors brought this breed of horse to the Americas. Herds of wild Andalusians soon became common throughout the southwest.

tribes used to increase their stock. The tribes that did not yet have horses got them by trading with other tribes. This was the start of the horse culture among the tribes of the Plains. By 1760, all the native peoples of the Plains as far north as Canada had horses.

In 1535, a Spanish soldier named Pedro de Mendoza brought an army of 2,000 men and about 100 horses to Argentina. There, he founded a settlement which later became the city of Buenos Aires. The Spanish abandoned the settlement after a few years, however, because of attacks by the native Charros and because of a lack of food. Some historians believe that herds of wild horses developed from some horses abandoned by Mendoza. Others believe that most of them descended from horses stolen by the native tribes or from horses brought to Chile and elsewhere in South America by the Spanish. By 1580, when the Spanish had taken over the area again, observers were reporting that many wild horses lived on the Pampas, the great plains of Argentina. In the next 20 years, the native peoples of Argentina and Paraguay would make changes to their lifestyle because of the horse.

As in North America, the Spaniards did not encourage the natives to use the horse. But the Indians learned how to use the animals anyway by observing the Spanish horsemen, working for them on breeding farms, and capturing their own wild horses. In both North and South America, one of the most powerful weapons of the Spanish had changed the Native American culture. ⑤

17

NATIVE AMERICAN LIFE

3 The Horse on the North American Plains

For 200 years, beginning in the mid–1700s, the Native Americans of the North American Plains had one of the world's most important horse cultures. The horse affected most aspects of their lives, including traveling, hunting, war, religion, and recreation. The horse even had an effect in the northwest as far as British Columbia, Canada. Before that, these tribes did not have much in common with the Plains tribes. Their lives centered around fishing and the forest. After the coming of the horse, however, their cultures changed in many ways, especially because they were able to take part in the buffalo hunt.

A Native American hunter prepares to kill a buffalo from horseback in this 1845 painting. The arrival of the horse in North America changed the culture of the Native Americans living on the plains by allowing them more freedom to hunt buffalo, bear, deer, elk, and other large game.

Native Americans built up their herds by rounding up wild horses into *corrals*, or by stealing them from settlers and other native tribes. Most tribes did not have a breeding program to improve the quality of their horses. An exception was the Nez Percé tribe of the northwestern United States, who lived just to the west of the Rocky

Mountains. They bred their horses in the area of the Palouse River. Because of this, the horses came to be known as Appaloosas. The Nez Percé bred their best horses to be useful for different jobs and for their unusual spotted coloring. **Geldings** were more popular for hunting and war than **stallions**. The native peoples believed that geldings were easier to handle and were faster than stallions. Except in the case of the Appaloosa, color was not too important, but most Native Americans liked the **paint** horse.

Training of horses usually started when the horse was about two years old. The most common method was to catch the horse by throwing a rope over its head. The man then approached the horse, talking to it all the time. Gradually, he put a **halter** on its head, which put pressure on its nose and neck. By running his hands over the horse, the man helped the horse get used to the smell and feel of humans. After leaning more and more heavily on the horse's back, the man would mount. By this time, the horse usually did not object much to having a person on its back. Another method used by the Hidatsa tribe, who lived near the Missouri River, was to drive a young horse into the water. While it was still in the water, a boy got on its back. Every time the horse reached the shore again, the boy would dismount. After repeating this several times, the young horse was quite tired. When it came out of the water for the last time, the boy stayed on its back.

Some tribes used saddles for riding—something that they had copied from the Spanish. More often, they went bareback or tied a

In the northwest, tribes such as the Salish and the Shoshoni got the horse by trading with the Comanche and the Ute. In the early fall, these tribes traveled east across the Rocky Mountains for the buffalo hunt. Most northwest tribes continued to gather fish, berries, and other traditional foods. The Nisqualli, in northwestern Washington, were the only Coast Salish people to get many horses. The Shuswap of British Columbia, an Interior Salish people, had horses by 1780, but used them mainly for travel.

By 1800, the Cayuse people of Oregon and Washington were so rich in horses that they dominated other tribes despite their small number of people. They no longer needed to fish, because they could trade horses for fish and other goods. The word "Cayuse" eventually came to mean a Native American horse.

pad to the horse's back. Women and older people often used saddles built on a wooden frame. Riders also used *stirrups* to improve their stability on the horse's back. They guided the horse using pressure from their knees and also with a simple *bridle*. Usually, they tied a rope around the horse's neck. If the rider fell off or had to dismount, he or she could then easily grab the horse by the rope.

In most tribes, children learned how to ride at an early age. Boys could ride well by the age of five or six. They learned riding skills that were useful in war and in hunting. They learned how to pick objects, and even people, up from the ground while the horse

A group of Native Americans have loaded all their belongings onto a travois in this 19th-century illustration. A horse pulled the travois, which was a simple frame often made of tepee poles. It enabled the Indians to easily move their belongings from camp to camp.

was galloping. Knowing how to ride was important for everyone because men, women, and children rode from place to place when moving camp.

The horse was also used for carrying goods when moving camp. A common method for moving goods around was the **travois**. Before acquiring the horse, the natives used the travois with dogs, but they could carry larger loads using horses. A travois was made of poles crossed in a V-shape and attached to the horse's shoulders. Where the poles extended behind the horse, there was a platform where items such as tepees, household goods, and even people could be placed. One observer described a Sioux horse pulling as many as four women and children on a travois. The travois poles usually doubled as tepee poles. After they started using the travois with horses, the Native Americans found they could make and carry larger tepees.

The horse allowed the tribes to hunt more effectively than before. In some tribes, before they had horses, hunters drove herds of buffalo into a pen with a cliff at one end, where the animals fell and broke their legs. They also surrounded herds on foot and then shot individual buffalos using the bow and arrow. After the coming of the horse, the tribes could more easily follow the herds, so meat was always available to them.

A hunting horse was one of the most valuable things that a person could own, as it had special qualities. The Blackfeet of Montana and Alberta, Canada, started training their hunting horses when the horses were four years old. The horse had to be willing to go close to the

23

buffalo so that its rider could get a good shot. The horse also learned to swerve away quickly when the hunter shot a buffalo. Otherwise, the wounded buffalo would turn on the horse and possibly gouge it with its sharp horns.

Some tribes hunted bareback, while others used a pad. The hunters guided their horses mainly by leg and knee pressure, as well as the

When the Plains Indians got horses, tribes such as the Sioux, Blackfeet, Crow, Cheyenne, Arapaho, Comanche, and Kiowa gave up their permanent villages. They moved regularly in order to follow the herds of buffalo.

rider's shifting weight. There were two main methods of horseback hunting. In the surround method, a group of hunters surrounded a herd of buffalo and rode towards them, shooting their arrows. In the chase method, individual hunters picked out a buffalo and raced after it, getting close enough for a good shot. Hunting was a risky business. Horses sometimes tripped and even broke their legs from stepping in a second, they became a target for the other tribe's arrows. Before going into battle, the warriors painted special designs on their horses. These designs might symbolize something like strength or speed, or they might have a religious meaning. Handprints were a common decoration. The Bannock tribe of southern Idaho painted their war horses with white clay. Other decorations included feathers and bear claw necklaces.

Most Native American tribes acquired a lot of their horses by stealing them from other tribes and from white settlers. However, trade was another way that horses spread from tribe to tribe. The tribes of the Pueblo Indians were among the first to acquire horses, and the animals spread in all directions from there. The eastern Plains tribes traded horses across the Mississippi River. The tribes to the east of the Mississippi then took on some of the characteristics of the Plains tribes. They would cross the Mississippi to take part in the buffalo hunts.

Tribes met in large groups for horse trading, especially in the summer. Trading or giving away horses was a sign of goodwill. Native American chiefs sometimes exchanged horses when they met to agree on a treaty. Some tribes counted their wealth in horses. The chiefs of certain tribes owned as many as 1,000 horses. Obviously, a horse was a valued gift. Young men often gave horses to their bride's father. The Lakota Sioux holy man Black Elk told the story of a young Lakota man called High Horse. He fell in love with a girl, but all he could get was four horses to give to her father, who would not accept them. High Horse and his friend attacked a Crow camp and stole about 100 horses. High Horse drove the horses back to his camp and stopped with them outside the father's tepee. According to Black Elk, "High Horse called out to him and asked if he thought maybe that would be enough

In horse raids and during battle, one of the greatest accomplishments of a warrior was "counting coup." Unarmed warriors tried to strike an armed enemy with a stick, called a coup stick, and hopefully get away unharmed. Counting coup brought great honor to a warrior. Among tribes such as the Hidatsa, warriors trained their horses to leap over a fallen enemy. As the horse leapt, the warrior tried to strike.

A mounted band of warriors goes on the warpath in this illustration. In Mexico and the American southwest, raiding parties often hoped to capture the horses of another tribe or of American or Mexican ranchers or settlers.

4 The Horse in the Southwest

The native peoples of Mexico and the American Southwest were the first to acquire the horse from the Spanish. In 1680, the Pueblo people of New Mexico drove out the Spanish. The Spanish left behind some horses, however, which the Pueblo took for themselves. In the history of the horse and the native peoples of North America, the Pueblo are most famous for trading the horse to the natives of the Plains. Though the horse did not become as useful to them as it did to the Plains tribes, the peoples of the southwest used the horse in such things as agriculture, war, and religion. They ranged over an area that included the modern-day states of Colorado, Arizona, New Mexico, Texas, and northern Mexico.

Some of the tribes in the southwest practiced something called "seasonal rounds." They moved to different territories during the year, depending on the time of year and the resources available. The horse was especially important to these people. Before the horse, they had moved slowly, using dogs to carry small loads. The horse allowed them to move more quickly and to carry larger loads. The southwest tribes relied heavily on trade. Because they could carry more trade goods and items for themselves using horses, their level of material comfort went up.

Among tribes such as the Apache, everyone could ride. Men and women traveled on horseback, and children learned to ride at an early age. Boys looked after the horses. Riding equipment was usually simple. Sometimes they used saddles, but often a pad or blanket was enough. For a bridle, they used a rope looped around the horse's jaw. The Dené of Arizona and New Mexico sometimes used more decorative gear to show their pride in their horses. If they could afford it, they used bridles with silver parts and well-made leather saddles. When using a saddle, they placed a rolled blanket behind the saddle. This was another custom borrowed from the Spanish riders in Mexico.

The southwest was drier and less grassy than the plains and had more mountains. Thus, the animals and plants of the southwest supported a different way of life for its inhabitants. Some of the tribes in the eastern areas of the southwest, including some Apache groups, took up buffalo hunting after the coming of the horse. Other tribes used the horse to hunt their traditional prey, including deer, antelope, and rabbit. Previously, they had hunted deer and antelope on foot, using bows and arrows. To kill rabbits, they used a throwing stick, similar to a spear. After acquiring the horse, their hunts became more productive.

The Native Americans in the southwest also used the horse for food, which the tribes in other parts of North America generally did not do. For some tribes, the horse was a common food.

A group of mounted Native Americans prepares to ford a river in this painting by Thomas Moran. The horse enabled Native American tribes of the Southwest to travel greater distances.

An Indian raises his arm in a peace sign in this 1908 illustration by Henry François Farny. This rider is seated in a saddle, which was uncommon among Native American horsemen.

Others ate horsemeat only occasionally. Many southwest tribes ate mostly vegetables, such as corn, beans, and squash. The Hopi, who were mainly vegetarian, would eat horsemeat if a horse died unexpectedly so as not to waste the meat. They also dried some of the meat for later use. The native peoples used the horse to herd sheep and goats. The horse also played a role in agriculture. For instance, the farmers used horses to trample grain so they could separate the seeds from the husks.

Horse raids were common among tribes such as the Apache, the Dené, and the Mescalero. In a raiding party, there were usually no more than three to ten people. The Apache sometimes had as many as 40 in one group. They went on foot, hoping to ride home on the horses they would take from another tribe or a settler's ranch. Raiders carried magic charms and used spells and prayers to protect themselves and to make sure that the raid would go well. The leader of a raid was supposed to be a man with "horse power," who had been given special power through a supernatural experience involving horses. Like the Plains tribes, the raiders in the southwest tried to steal several horses quietly without losing any of their men or getting injured. When they raided Spanish settlements for horses, especially in New Mexico, they watched the pastures and stole horses when no one was guarding them.

Several tribes used the horse in open warfare. The Apache fought many wars against other tribes, revolts against the Spanish, and raids into Mexico. War bands were much larger than raiding parties. Warriors fighting on horseback used the bow and arrow. The Apache also used armor made from bone or thick animal skins on their horses. However, not all southwestern tribes with horses used the horse for fighting. The Yuma of Arizona and California, who had some horses by the late 1700s, believed that using the horse in battle gave them an unfair advantage.

Horses were an important trade item for the peoples of the southwest. Villages and tribes met during the summer to trade and socialize. Besides horses, they also traded items such as blankets and pottery. The Apaches and the Zuñis met once in a while for trade and

5 The Horse in South America

The horse culture of South America was mainly located in the southern half of South America, an area called Patagonia. The areas affected by the horse included Argentina, Paraguay, and southern Brazil. The horse also had some impact on the native peoples in Peru and Chile, but not as much as in Patagonia.

The wild horses of South America were known as *baguales*. The word may come from the Spanish word for horse, *caballo*. There was not as much color variety among these horses as there was among the wild horses in North America. Most of the wild horses in South America were brown in color. The native peoples in South America did very little breeding. They acquired most of their horses by raiding Spanish settlements and other tribes and also by capturing wild horses.

When the native peoples of Patagonia began to acquire the horse around the early 1700s, their way of life changed a great deal. As was

This mounted gaucho is wearing the traditional costume of the Pampas. Gauchos were expert horsemen who used their mounts to herd cattle in the present-day countries of Argentina, Paraguay, and Brazil.

After Christopher Columbus explored South and Central America during his third voyage, Spain began sending soldiers to conquer the land. This 17th-century map, inscribed in Latin, shows the regions where the Spaniards settled. The clothing and activities of the natives of South America are shown in the lower left corner of the map. Use of the horse soon spread throughout the area of Spanish influence.

the case with other tribes, they could move around much more easily and carry more belongings with them. They were also able to travel farther to collect different plants for food and medicine. At first, they used very little equipment. They went bareback and often they did not even use a bridle. Later, when they started to use the bridle, it was just a simple rope running through the horse's mouth. They also used bridles that controlled the horse by putting pressure on its nose. The native peoples copied saddles from Spanish models. The Tehuelche of southern Patagonia used bunches of reeds tied together and covered with blankets.

The famous horsemen of South America, the *gauchos*, were usually part native and part Spanish. They herded horses and cattle on the Pampas in northern Argentina. Their way of life combined native traditions and Spanish culture. Their weapons for hunting were much like the weapons used by the native peoples.

43

After the coming of the horse, the native South Americans continued to hunt the same animals as they had in the past. These included the guanaco, an animal related to the camel, and the rhea, a flightless bird like the ostrich. They also hunted deer, wild cats, and the peccary, a kind of wild pig. Before getting the horse, the natives hunted these animals on foot, using the bow and arrow. After acquiring the horse, they returned to using the bola, an ancient weapon made of hard balls tied to leather ropes. During a hunt, the horseback hunters started in a long crescent formation, gradually closing it to make a circle around a herd of animals. Then they closed in on the animals,

NATIVE AMERICAN LIFE

throwing their bolas. The weapons would wrap around the animals' legs, bringing them to the ground. The hunters also killed animals with a blow on the head from one hard ball attached to a rope. They often brought dogs with them on hunts, but the bolas worked so well that they usually did not need to use the dogs.

When they started hunting with horses, many of the tribes stopped fishing and growing their own crops. This was the case with the Tehuelche and also the Abipón, who lived to the north of the Tehuelche on the Gran Chaco. Some tribes, including the Mapuche and the Puelche, ate quite a lot of horsemeat. They usually used the mares for food, rather than the male horses.

Warfare on horseback changed the tribes' culture a great deal. Wars between the tribes and among bands within the tribes were common. For instance, native bands in the Gran Chaco fought each other to expand their territories. The Tehuelche fought against each other in bands of 500 to 1,000. The tribes were able to move around more with horses, and this often resulted in different tribes' territories overlapping. Horses and increased warfare changed the social classes within tribes. The people with the most horses were the most powerful. The nobles and warriors were above the servants and

This illustration shows South American natives hunting guanacos with the bola, a weapon they could throw from horseback to entangle the legs of their prey.

slaves, who included people captured in battle. The war leader

became the most powerful man in a native band.

The native peoples fought on horseback with lances that were

about 18 feet long, as well as with bolas and swords. They made

helmets, armor, and shields out of thick animal skins. Their custom

A Brazilian boy rides a dappled horse bareback on the island of Marajos, in the Para district of Brazil. The arrival of the horse changed the lives of the natives of South America as much as it had changed the culture of the natives of North America.

when attacking a Spanish settlement or another native group was to attack by surprise, often early in the morning. They took a large number of horses along. When the horses they were riding got tired, they could

During the civil wars of the 1800s in South America, some of the gauchos fought on horseback as a group called the "montonera."

change to fresh ones. A warrior could hang off the side of his horse so as to be almost invisible from the other side. Before an attack, a person watching from the distance might think there were only a few riders driving a large number of riderless horses. Then the warriors swung themselves up onto their horses and rushed in for the attack.

Horses made trade between native groups much easier, since it allowed them to travel more freely. The horses themselves were important trade items, as were blankets and cloaks made out of horse skins and guanaco skins. In the eastern Pampas, the Mapuche tribe dominated the horse trade. In the 1800s, an observer described trading between the Tehuelche and the Manzanero, who lived to the north of the Tehuelche. They traded horses, woven blankets, and silver ornaments. Horse trading also allowed different tribes to get horses that were useful for different purposes. The Manzanero had horses that were better looking and faster for racing, but they did not have the endurance of the horses the Tehuelche used for hunting.

47

Here, too, horses were common marriage gifts from the groom's family to the bride's family. The groom would ride on his best horse to the home of the bride's family to give them his gifts. Parents gave horses to their young children. The horses then belonged entirely to the children. The parents were not allowed to take them away or give them to someone else. During ceremonies of meeting, tribes gave horses as gifts to each other.

Like the other Native Americans, the native peoples of South America killed horses at funerals. At a chief's funeral, four horses were killed and their skins were stuffed. Then they were propped up at the four corners of the grave. At the funeral of an ordinary man, his horse was killed, stuffed, and propped up facing the grave. In both cases, the people ate the horsemeat after killing the horses. Among the Tehuelche, horse sacrifices were common on many occasions. For instance, they might kill some mares after a child had been hurt. The sacrifice was to thank the gods that the child was still alive, and to keep the child from getting hurt again. In fact, the southernmost Tehuelche tribes used horses mainly for sacrifice and less for other purposes.

Horse racing was a popular form of recreation among the native peoples in South America as well. The races usually took place between two horses, ridden bareback, over about four miles. Races took place between native bands and also between various tribes. For example, the Tehuelche and the Araucanians, who lived on the west coast, met to race their horses. Peoples sometimes had spells put on their horses before a race to help them win.

The Native Americans of South America took good care of their horses, too. A writer who spent time with the Tehuelche in the 1800s commented: "One rarely sees a horse amongst the Indians that is not perfectly quiet…although if a white man approaches or attempts to catch them they show signs of fear and temper." He also noted that the horses tended to be thin because they ate only grass, but that their owners gave them the best care if they were injured. According to this writer, there was "a sort of instinctive mutual bond between the Indians and their horses." §

A Native American cowboy attempts to rope a steer from horseback in a modern-day rodeo. Although horsemanship remains a prized skill, Native American culture is no longer centered on the horse.

6 The Decline of the Native American Horse Culture

The horse culture started to decline in the Americas during the late 1800s. In North America, this decline happened mainly because of the near-disappearance of the buffalo from the Plains, and also because the government wanted to force the Native Americans onto reservations. In South America, Europeans limited the freedom of the native peoples and eventually wiped out most of their horses.

In the mid-1800s, the American West became an important destination. The Gold Rush brought thousands of people to California. However, even after the Gold Rush slowed down, people continued to come west because they saw it as a land of opportunity. Also, *stockmen* wanted the Plains as a place to farm and raise cattle.

In the 1850s and 1860s, railroad companies pushed westward. By 1865, the Pacific Railroad Company had reached Kansas City. Suddenly, it was easy for white hunters to kill buffalo. They saw several advantages in doing so. The skins and meat could be sold at a profit, and less buffalo meant more grazing land for cattle. Also, if the buffalo were killed off, it would mean an end to the traditional native way of life on the Plains. The government and the stockmen saw the Native Americans as a threat and an obstacle to their quest for land.

The U.S. government posted groups of *cavalry* across the Plains to stop the Native Americans from causing trouble. Gradually, the army forced the natives in different areas onto reservations. When they did this, they often killed or took away their horses. In 1877, the Nez Percé refused to go onto a reservation. Led by Chief Joseph, they retreated from the U.S. Army for about 1,300 miles, taking their Appaloosa horses with them. When they finally surrendered in Montana, the army captured the horses. They sold them off or killed them. Similar events took place in different parts of North America. In some places, many natives died of starvation because of the disappearance of the buffalo. Even if the army had not taken away or killed so many of the horses, the horses would no longer have been as useful to the native tribes because the great herds of buffalo were gone.

"We gave up all our horses—over 1,100—and all our saddles—over 100—and we have not heard from them since. Somebody has got our horses."

—Chief Joseph in 1879

In South America, the 1800s were also a bad time for the native inhabitants. European illnesses and alcohol had a terrible effect on the native peoples. In the second half of the century, European colonists divided up the Pampas and other areas into large ranches. Instead of working independently with horses, as they had in the past, the gauchos now had to work on the ranches. European ranchers killed most of the wild stock to make room for their own horses and cattle. Some native tribes disappeared almost entirely because of wars with other tribes and European expansion. Others became slaves and workers for the Europeans or went onto reservations.

Today, Native Americans in the American southwest still use horses. However, they are just as likely to use modern forms of transportation, such as this Jeep, to get where they are going.

A group of Native Americans takes their horses onto the reservation in this illustration from a 19th-century book. When the Native Americans were forced onto reservations by the U.S. government, their horse-centered culture began to decline.

The native horse culture of the Americas is long past its most important period, which lasted from around the early 1600s to the mid–1800s. However, some aspects of the horse culture still exist among Native Americans today. They have made important contributions to the world of horsemanship. For example, the U.S. government did not completely wipe out the Appaloosa breed. In the 1930s, breeders used a few remaining Appaloosas to revive the breed. Today, the Appaloosa is one of the world's most popular riding horses. In South America, the modern Criollo horse is a descendant of the horses used by the Native Americans and the gauchos. There are thousands of wild horses in North America, as well as in some smaller areas of South America. Tribes such as the Guajira in South America and the Dené in the southern United States still use horses in ranching, for traveling, and in traditional ceremonies and parades. Because of the importance of cars, trucks, and other motor vehicles today, however, horses all over the world and in Native American society are used mainly for pleasure and as a way to remember the past. In their folklore, their art, and their use of the horse today, Native Americans remember the time when the horse meant power and riches to them, as well as being a friend and a gift from the gods. §

The official Appaloosa breed registry is the third largest in the world today. The Pony of the Americas, a cross between the Appaloosa and the Shetland Pony, has the same coat patterns as the Appaloosa.

55

Chronology

1494 On his second voyage to the West Indies, Christopher Columbus brings 30 horses with him; breeding farms are set up on the islands.

1519 Hernán Cortés sails from Cuba to Mexico with a large army and 16 horses.

1531–32 Francisco Pizarro brings the horse to Peru.

1535 Pedro de Mendoza brings the horse to Argentina; herds of wild horses eventually spread across the Pampas plains.

1542 The Spanish give horses to Aztec chieftains in Mexico, who are their allies, to use in war.

c. 1567–79 Use of the horse among the native peoples of Mexico becomes common.

c. 1590 Native peoples in South America are capturing wild horses and riding them.

c. 1600–1630 The Spanish breed horses in the missions of the Rio Grande Valley; they train some Native Americans in the care and use of horses; some natives take horses and escape with them.

1680 The Pueblo people force the Spanish out of New Mexico; the Spanish leave behind many horses, which the Pueblo trade to the Native Americans of the southern Plains.

c. 1700 The Tehuelche people of South America are using the horse for hunting and for transportation.

c. 1754 The Blackfeet Confederacy in Montana and Alberta is using horses in large numbers.

c. 1760 All North American Plains tribes have horses.

1865 The Pacific Railroad Company reaches Kansas City; stockmen start killing off the buffalo in large numbers.

c. 1874 The tribes of the North American Plains own about 160,000 horses.

1877 The U.S. government forces the Nez Percé onto a reservation and takes away their Appaloosa horses.

1938 The Appaloosa Horse Club is formed in Moscow, Idaho, to revive the Appaloosa breed.

2003 There are an estimated 3 million Native Americans living in the United States and Canada.

Glossary

baguale wild horse in South America descended from Spanish horses.

bay common horse color (brown with black mane, tail, and legs).

break to tame a horse so that it can be ridden.

bridle a piece of equipment fastened around a horse's head to control it while riding.

cavalry soldiers on horseback.

conquistador any one of the Spanish leaders of the conquest of the Americas in the 1500s.

corral an enclosure for holding animals.

enmity a strong feeling of dislike or even hatred.

gaucho South American horseman, usually part Spanish and part Native American.

gelding a neutered male horse.

halter a piece of equipment fastened around a horse's head so that it can be led with a rope.

mare a female horse.

mission a religious settlement built by people who want to bring their religion to others.

mustang a wild horse in North America and Mexico descended from Spanish horses.

paint horse color consisting of more than one color, usually white and another dark color.

provisions a supply of food and materials.

stallion an unneutered male horse.

stirrups loops hanging off a saddle for a rider's feet.

stockman a farmer who herds cattle.

tepee a round structure, pointed at the top, used by Native American tribes in North America.

travois two poles tied together in a "V" shape and attached to a horse to drag loads.

Further Reading

Barclay, Harold. *The Role of the Horse in Man's Culture.* London: J.A. Allen & Co, 1980.

Clutton-Brock, Juliet. *Horse Power: A History of the Horse and the Donkey in Human Society.* Cambridge: Harvard University Press, 1992.

Irwin, Stephen R. *Hunters of the Buffalo.* Surrey, B.C.: Hancock House Publishers, 1984.

Ed. McEwan, Colin, et al. *Patagonia: Natural History, Prehistory and Ethnography at the Uttermost End of the Earth.* Princeton: Princeton University Press, 1997.

Nies, Judith. *Native American History.* New York: Ballantine Books, 1996.

Pritzker, Barry M. *A Native American Encyclopedia: History, Culture, and Peoples.* New York: Oxford University Press, 2000.

Ed. Salomon, Frank and Stuart B. Schwartz. *The Cambridge History of the Native Peoples of the Americas: South America* (Vol. 1 and 2). Cambridge: Cambridge University Press, 1999.

NATIVE AMERICAN LIFE

Internet Resources

http://www.bcc.cc.tx.us/acdem/social/mdwlwn/1302/doc04.htm

This site provides an excerpt of speeches made by Chief Joseph regarding his thoughts on the takeover of Indian lands.

http://www.justacriollo.com

This Web site on the South American Criollo horse is aimed at providing information on its origin and history, the characteristics of this hardy animal, and the areas in which it excels.

http://www.pbs.org/wildhorses/wh_man/wh_indians.html

Information on how mustangs first came to America, their relationship with man, and prospects for their future.

NATIVE AMERICAN LIFE

Index

Picture Credits